Meeting the North Korean Nuclear Challenge

*Report of an Independent Task Force
Sponsored by the
Council on Foreign Relations*

Morton I. Abramowitz and James T. Laney,
Co-Chairs
Eric Heginbotham, Project Director

The Council on Foreign Relations is dedicated to increasing America's understanding of the world and contributing ideas to U.S. foreign policy. The Council accomplishes this mainly by promoting constructive debates, clarifying world issues, producing reports, and publishing *Foreign Affairs*, the leading journal on global issues. The Council is host to the widest possible range of views, but an advocate of none, though its research fellows and Independent Task Forces do take policy positions.

THE COUNCIL TAKES NO INSTITUTIONAL POSITION ON POLICY ISSUES AND HAS NO AFFILIATION WITH THE U.S. GOVERNMENT. ALL STATEMENTS OF FACT AND EXPRESSIONS OF OPINION CONTAINED IN ALL ITS PUBLICATIONS ARE THE SOLE RESPONSIBILITY OF THE AUTHOR OR AUTHORS.

The Council will sponsor an Independent Task Force when (1) an issue of current and critical importance to U.S. foreign policy arises, and (2) it seems that a group diverse in backgrounds and perspectives may, nonetheless, be able to reach a meaningful consensus on a policy through private and nonpartisan deliberations. Typically, a Task Force meets between two and five times over a brief period to ensure the relevance of its work.

Upon reaching a conclusion, a Task Force issues a report, and the Council publishes its text and posts it on the Council website, www.cfr.org. Task Force reports can take three forms: (1) a strong and meaningful policy consensus, with Task Force members endorsing the general policy thrust and judgments reached by the group, though not necessarily every finding and recommendation; (2) a report stating the various policy positions, each as sharply and fairly as possible; or (3) a "Chair's Report," where Task Force members who agree with the Chair's report may associate themselves with it, while those who disagree may submit dissenting statements. Upon reaching a conclusion, a Task Force may also ask individuals who were not members of the Task Force to associate themselves with the Task Force report to enhance its impact. All Task Force reports "benchmark" their findings against current administration policy in order to make explicit areas of agreement and disagreement. The Task Force is solely responsible for its report. The Council takes no institutional position.

For further information about the Council or this Task Force, please write the Council on Foreign Relations, 58 East 68th Street, New York, NY 10021, or call the Director of Communications at 212-434-9400. Visit our website at www.cfr.org.

CONTENTS

FOREWORD

For years, it has been hard to think of a state more troublesome than North Korea, in terms of treatment of its citizens, development of armed forces greatly disproportionate to its size and economy, involvement in dangerous sales of military technology, and perhaps involvement in terrorism as well. Now that North Korea has reembarked on a nuclear development program that could lead to a nuclear weapons arsenal for itself and for sale to others, it has become downright dangerous to its neighbors and to the United States. The diplomatic, economic, and military keys to reducing that danger have been elusive, so at this ever-more-threatening moment, the Council on Foreign Relations once again turned to its Korea Task Force—which in the past has been so helpful to the United States and to South Korea in developing good policy on this problem—for another try at recommending solutions.

The Task Force, first formed in 1997, continues to be chaired by two of America's foremost foreign policy and security experts, Ambassador Morton I. Abramowitz, former assistant secretary of state for intelligence and research, and James T. Laney, former U.S. ambassador to the Republic of Korea (ROK, or South Korea). Task Force members include leading experts, both policymakers and academics, on northeast Asian and nonproliferation policy issues. Eric Heginbotham, senior fellow in Asia studies at the Council, serves as project director.

This Task Force report is especially timely in light of recent developments. North Korea has acknowledged that it has a secret highly enriched uranium (HEU) program, withdrawn from the nuclear Nonproliferation Treaty (NPT), expelled inspectors from the International Atomic Energy Agency (IAEA), asserted that it has nuclear weapons, and declared that it is reprocessing spent nuclear fuel. In considering how best to confront these challenges, the Task Force report makes the following major points and associated recommendations:

First, the Task Force argues that the United States needs to restore a healthy alliance and forge a common strategy with South Korea. No strategy is likely to work unless these two traditional allies are in lockstep.

Second, the Task Force believes the United States must form a broader coalition. It urges the administration to establish a policy around which American partners can rally. The active participation of friends and allies in the region, including China, Japan, and Russia, in addition to South Korea, will be critical to a successful resolution of the crisis. And the Task Force believes that the best way to achieve allied unity would be for the United States to agree to enter into serious negotiations with Pyongyang in exchange for a commitment from U.S. partners to take tougher measures should negotiations fail.

Third, the Task Force believes that the crisis may be coming to a head and that, although a broad settlement of all nuclear and missile concerns would be essential to any long-term agreement, the United States should first propose an interim agreement as an immediate test of North Korean intentions. Such an agreement would require Pyongyang to readmit inspectors, freeze its nuclear reactors and reprocessing facilities, and turn over its spent nuclear fuel. In return, the United States would pledge not to attack the North as long as the agreement remained in effect and would agree not to stop other countries from providing assistance to the North.

The Task Force also recommends the appointment of a special, high-level full-time coordinator for Korean issues to help define and coordinate U.S. policy, work with regional partners to establish a unified policy approach, and, at the appropriate time, negotiate with senior North Korean leaders.

Finally, the Task Force suggests the United States should develop an agreed set of tough contingency actions to be taken if negotiations fail.

The Task Force is not sanguine about the prospects for reaching either an interim agreement or a more comprehensive settlement, but its members believe that North Korea must be tested. There is some chance that negotiations will succeed and a peaceful end to the crisis may be found. Just as important, the United States cannot expect the full support of potential regional partners on other approaches if it does not first test the North.

My deep gratitude goes to the co-chairs, Morton I. Abramowitz and James T. Laney, for their dedication to this Task Force over the course of six years and to the project director, Council Senior Fellow Eric Heginbotham, for his tireless efforts to produce a timely and important report.

Leslie H. Gelb
President
Council on Foreign Relations
June 2003

ACKNOWLEDGMENTS

The Task Force has spent the last several months tracking and try-ing to make sense of a rapidly changing situation on the Korean Peninsula. In this effort, we were fortunate to have had as co-chairs Morton I. Abramowitz and James T. Laney, two of America's fore-most experts on Korean security and foreign policy issues. They have been the leaders of the Task Force since 1997. In addition to sharing their experience and expertise, the co-chairs devoted countless hours to organizing and overseeing the Task Force effort, keeping the project on track, and moving it forward despite shifting conditions on the ground in Asia.

The whole effort would have been impossible without the active participation and hard work of the Task Force members, who bring together a truly unique body of knowledge about Korean issues. Task Force meetings were conducted with an air of openness and collegiality that should serve as a model for collaborative work. Special thanks are due to the Task Force members for their willingness to read multiple drafts on short notice and respond with detailed comments and suggestions. Several members also shared their expertise with me individually, providing extended tutorials on everything from the North Korean economy, to social and atti-tudinal change in South Korea, to the history of U.S.-Korea pol-icy and the record of the Agreed Framework.

The observers on the Task Force remained strictly neutral regarding the report's content but nevertheless generously shared their time, briefing the group on U.S. policy toward Korea. The Task Force also continued to benefit from a strong relationship with the Seoul Forum. In February 2003, we enjoyed an opportunity to exchange views with Kim Kyung-Won, Lee Hong-Koo, and Han Sung-Joo, who visited under the Forum's auspices.

Lee Feinstein, the director of strategic policy at the Council, not only provided administrative guidance throughout the process; he also took an active hand in shaping the substance of Task

Force discussions. Earl Carr, research associate at the Council, was instrumental in finding and organizing large amounts of data, bringing order to the project. Jessica Gingerich, a special assistant at the Century Foundation, assisted with the drafting and editorial process. The Council staff in New York provided strong support throughout the effort. Patricia Dorff, Lisa Shields, and Marie Strauss were standouts, though certainly not the only individuals who contributed to the final product.

The Korea Foundation deserves great thanks for its generous support of the Task Force's work, and we are indebted to the Arthur Ross Foundation for its general support of Council Task Forces.

Finally, the Task Force owes a deep debt of gratitude to Council President Leslie H. Gelb for his steadfast commitment to the group and its mission over the years. I owe him my personal thanks for giving me the opportunity to work with such a fine group of individuals as well as for his kind encouragement and guidance throughout the process. Given the strength of the Task Force members, the depth of staff support, and the outstanding leadership provided by Les Gelb and Lee Feinstein at the Council and Morton Abramowitz and James Laney within the Task Force, it should be obvious that any shortcomings in the report lie completely with me.

Eric Heginbotham
Project Director

EXECUTIVE SUMMARY

DPRK Nuclear Capabilities

Over the past two years, North Korea (the Democratic People's Republic of Korea, or DPRK) has advanced its nuclear weapons program and increasingly emphasized its need for a nuclear capability. Since October 2002, when it admitted having a clandestine program to make highly enriched uranium (HEU), the DPRK has withdrawn from the nuclear Nonproliferation Treaty (NPT), asserted it possesses nuclear weapons, and announced that it is reprocessing its spent nuclear fuel. In May 2003, Pyongyang declared that its 1992 "denuclearization" pledge with South Korea was dead. North Korean violations of the Agreed Framework, the basis of U.S.-North Korean relations since 1994, have left that agreement in tatters.

North Korean assertions cannot all be independently confirmed by U.S. intelligence. Even more uncertain are North Korean intentions. Some observers believe North Korea is seeking a serious nuclear weapons capability as its only means of deterring an American attack. Others believe that North Korea is interested in negotiations and prepared to bargain away its nuclear capabilities in exchange for American security guarantees, diplomatic relations with the United States, and economic assistance (from either the United States or other countries).

Whatever Pyongyang's motivations, recent events point to North Korea becoming a more capable—and avowed—nuclear state. The United States has not yet found a way to prevent this eventuality.

U.S.-DPRK Interactions

The Bush administration completed its first review of U.S. policy toward the Korean Peninsula in June 2001. The review left the door open for talks with Pyongyang but stipulated that any agreement would have to address a broad range of issues, including North Korea's nuclear program, its ballistic missile and conventional threats, an accelerated schedule for its compliance with International Atomic Energy Agency (IAEA) safeguards, and human rights concerns.

The few high-level meetings between DPRK and U.S. officials since the review have not constituted or led to serious negotiations. The North showed little interest in the comprehensive American proposal put forth in June 2001, and the United States was then prepared only to present its position. In October 2002, when Assistant Secretary of State for East Asian and Pacific Affairs James Kelly visited Pyongyang, North Korea confirmed its covert pursuit of an HEU program, an admission that ended any discussion of proposals for a settlement of nuclear or other issues. In the two sides' second meeting in April 2003 in Beijing (a meeting that also included China), the United States and North Korea presented almost mirror image proposals on the nuclear issue. The DPRK insisted on U.S. security assurances, among other things, before it would address its nuclear weapons program, and the United States insisted on the "irrevocable and verifiable" dismantlement of the North's HEU program and the refreezing of other aspects of its nuclear weapons program before the United States would engage on other issues.

U.S. Policy Approach

Although the Bush administration abandoned the Clinton administration's engagement policy, it is not clear what has replaced it. Policymaking has often been confusing to outsiders, largely because of continuing deep divisions and discordant voices at high levels within the U.S. government. One camp favors continuing negotiations with the North on a verifiable end to its nuclear program as part of a larger settlement covering concerns from the conventional military threat to human rights. The other camp favors a policy of political and economic isolation and strangulation that hopefully will lead to the collapse of the decrepit North Korean regime. President Bush has apparently chosen so far to effectively follow a policy of isolation, punctuated by occasional, mostly fruitless meetings with the North.

After North Korea admitted its HEU program, the United States first insisted that the North must take visible measures to dismantle its nuclear program before negotiations could take place. The administration later softened this position somewhat but insisted—quite correctly—that the North Korean nuclear problem was the concern of all powers in the region and that the issue had to be resolved on a multilateral basis. South Korea (the Republic of Korea, or ROK), China, Japan, and Russia all have vested interests in the stability of the Korean Peninsula and therefore should have a stake in measures to deal with the crisis. The United States has achieved some success with this approach. Its regional partners have expressly stated that a nuclear North is unacceptable. China was instrumental in bringing the DPRK to the trilateral talks in April 2003. Beijing's reluctance to see the peninsula go nuclear and its fear that the United States would take military action have motivated it to pursue an active role in seeking a solution. Japan, initially reluctant to take forceful action, has recently been leaning toward tougher measures against the North and has slowed remittances to Pyongyang from North Koreans living in Japan. Russia has warned North Korea to abandon its nuclear program. The ROK has moved to shore up its relations with the United States, and South Korean President Roh Moo-Hyun declared recently that the South will "not tolerate" North Korean nuclear weapons. Yet none of this has stopped North Korea's nuclear efforts.

The Problem of Allies

Despite some convergence of positions within the camp of nations allied with the United States, significant differences remain, limiting the effectiveness of policies adopted by each country. Washington favors a policy of isolation, while Seoul pursues one of conditional engagement. American friends and allies in the region part ways with the United States over how to manage the nuclear crisis and ultimately induce change in the North. America's regional partners fear that the United States will attack North Korean nuclear facilities, unleashing war on the peninsula. Intensive U.S. diplomacy with these states has won support for putting additional economic pressure on the North. Nevertheless, all of them, especially South Korea and China, tend to oppose anything resembling comprehensive sanctions for fear that an embargo would lead to war, as North Korea has threatened.

What the regional partners do agree on is that the United States should seriously negotiate with Pyongyang in the hope of reaching a peaceful resolution to the crisis or, at the very least, testing North Korean intentions. Although desirous of being included in the talks, on balance U.S. partners are far less concerned with being involved in multilateral negotiations than they are in ensuring that real negotiations—multilateral or bilateral—take place and that Washington and Pyongyang engage each other directly. The United States has not persuaded its regional partners that it is serious about negotiations, which has made securing their approval for a significantly tougher position difficult if not impossible. If negotiations fail or U.S. intelligence should confirm that North Korea has reprocessed its spent nuclear fuel, it is uncertain whether U.S. allies would be willing to put significantly greater pressure on North Korea.

What to Do

The Task Force believes that the United States is now facing a fundamentally different reality on the Korean Peninsula, one that constitutes a genuine crisis. We believe it is increasingly likely that North Korea can and will move to produce additional nuclear weapons material. We are unable to rule out that it seeks to hold off the United States until it is successful. The situation has drifted toward one in which the United States may have little choice but to live with a North Korea with more nuclear weapons and to find ways to prevent the North from exporting its fissile material. The Task Force believes the United States should strenuously try to prevent these outcomes. The best means of achieving this, the Task Force believes, is by trying to unite U.S. allies around a common policy. The best way to accomplish that, in turn, is to negotiate a verifiable nuclear settlement with the North and demand in return that America's regional partners adopt a tougher posture should negotiations fail. Even this option may not be available if North Korea has already reprocessed its spent fuel.

Specifically, the Task Force recommends the following:

- *Restore greater harmony in U.S.-ROK relations.* The U.S. and South Korean governments should mend their alliance and bolster public support for their larger relationship. The May 2003 meeting of the two presidents was an important step forward, as was the establishment of an interagency team to deal with problems in the alliance. Much work remains to be done. In the short term, this will require reestablishing greater support for the alliance among the South Korean public. Dealing with long-term issues will entail a more thorough examination of fundamental questions, including whether and in what configuration U.S. forces should remain in South Korea. We propose a high-level bilateral body to produce a program of both short- and long-term measures.

- *Enunciate a clear policy and build a strong coalition.* The Bush administration needs to establish a unified policy toward North Korea, one that will encourage America's partners to take greater responsibility for a resolution of the nuclear issue and to be prepared to take more forceful measures if necessary. A senior official should be assigned full-time responsibility for coordinating U.S. policy, dealing with the allies, and negotiating with North Korea.

- *Engage in serious, early, and direct negotiations with North Korea.* The Task Force believes that this will be indispensable in achieving allied unity and testing Pyongyang's intentions. America's partners in the region are unlikely to sign on to any policy of coercive measures that does not first test North Korea's repeated statements that it seeks a negotiated settlement of the nuclear and missile issues, and they may not do so even then. Without such an effort, the United States will find it difficult to take tougher measures and not have them undermined by allied disunity. We believe these discussions should take place in a forum where China, South Korea, Japan, and Russia also participate, but the United States is not likely to win the support of its allies if it precludes bilateral negotiations.

- *Develop a short-term proposal to test North Korean intentions.* An interim proposal, supported by the four major regional powers (the United States, South Korea, China, and Japan)—plus, if possible, Russia—would have the DPRK freeze its nuclear reactors and reprocessing facilities. Pyongyang must also re-admit inspectors and account for and turn over all spent nuclear fuel rods, as well as any plutonium separated from those rods. The United States, in exchange, would provide assurances that it will not attack North Korea and agree not to object to foreign assistance by other countries for as long as the interim agreement remains in effect. The primary purpose of this proposal would be to quickly test North Korea's intentions to stop its nuclear program.

- *Redouble efforts with China to pressure North Korea.* Given its unique relationship with the DPRK, China is a critical player in attempts to resolve the nuclear issue peacefully. It must take greater responsibility for getting North Korea to stop its nuclear program. The United States should enlist China in a combined effort to test North Korean intentions in exchange for a stronger commitment from Beijing to place an embargo on North Korea if Pyongyang fails to negotiate in good faith.

- *Contingencies.* Should negotiations fail and North Korea reprocess its spent fuel or test a nuclear weapon, the United States should seek to secure more meaningful sanctions and consider imposing a blockade designed to intercept nuclear and other illicit or deadly exports. Allied support would be critical.

TASK FORCE REPORT

INTRODUCTION

The situation on the Korean Peninsula has changed dramatically since the Task Force issued its last report almost two years ago:

- North Korea (the Democratic People's Republic of Korea, or DPRK) has asserted it has nuclear weapons. It stands on the brink of dramatically expanding its nuclear capabilities, and its threats to do so have escalated tensions in the area and raised fears of renewed hostilities. Its media constantly proclaims that the United States is intent on destroying the North Korean state. After a major diplomatic effort over several years to improve its standing in the world, Pyongyang has withdrawn from the nuclear Nonproliferation Treaty (NPT), declared the 1992 North-South nonnuclear pledge "nullified," and distanced itself from the world community.

- The Agreed Framework, the basis of U.S.-North Korean relations since 1994, lies in tatters. No serious dialogue between Washington and Pyongyang about resolving differences has taken place since the Bush administration took office. The latest talks in Beijing have produced uncertainty about whether North Korea has reprocessed its spent nuclear fuel rods as well as about what will be the next steps toward resolving the impasse.

- U.S. relations with South Korea (the Republic of Korea, or ROK) have become strained, in large part over basic differences about how to deal with North Korea. Similar differences also exist between the United States and other nations. Despite a variety of joint bilateral and multilateral statements with allies, no real common strategy toward North Korea has emerged.

- The United States has elevated China—North Korea's principal benefactor—to the role of major partner in trying to stop Pyongyang's nuclear weapons program.

The nuclear stakes have been widely discussed and could include:

- *Proliferation from North Korea.* Pyongyang might sell fissile material, nuclear technology, or completed weapons to any state or nonstate actor with money. It has little else to export.

- *An emboldened North Korea.* Pyongyang might believe that a growing nuclear arsenal gives it greater coercive leverage. It might therefore be emboldened to demand concessions from South Korea and other countries in the region and from the United States.

- *Secondary proliferation effects.* Neighbors that are currently satisfied with their nonnuclear status might feel less secure and consider a change in policy. Although any outcome is far from preordained, advocates of a stronger independent military posture in Japan and South Korea could push for change in those countries' nonnuclear posture. More generally, the global NPT regime would be weakened.

The outcome of the nuclear issue will heavily affect the region and America's role and military presence in it. Given public sentiment in South Korea, any military action by the United States against North Korean nuclear facilities without the support of the ROK could rupture the U.S.-ROK alliance. The nuclear issue has already accelerated discussions about reducing the size and footprint of U.S. forces in South Korea. Japan feels increasingly vulnerable in the face of North Korea's nuclear and missile capabilities. China is concerned about North Korea's behavior, as the potential for violence on the peninsula complicates efforts to maintain a calm external environment in which to pursue economic development and could affect the political position of the new, generally pro-reform leadership under Hu Jintao.

The Korean nuclear crisis is moving toward a dangerous denouement. North Korea is edging away from its stated eagerness (whether sincere or not) to negotiate a solution to both sides' security concerns and is increasingly emphasizing the deterrent value of "powerful weapons" and the virtues of its military-first policies. The Bush administration may be headed toward a strategy of containment rather than one designed to prevent the North from acquiring additional nuclear capabilities. U.S. partners in the region have not signed on to an aggressive containment campaign, in part because of the perceived risks of war inherent in any such policies and in part because they believe the North's willingness to negotiate a peaceful resolution of the issue has not been tested.

The United States could face a serious crisis with grave consequences and, potentially, few allies. The Task Force believes that the United States should move expeditiously to unify its regional partners by establishing a North Korea policy around which they can be persuaded to rally.

This report focuses on the nuclear dilemma posed by North Korea. It reviews how the United States got to the present crisis; assesses North Korea's situation and intentions; analyzes the policies of the United States, ROK, and other major regional players; and makes recommendations for dealing with North Korea.

WHERE ARE WE?

The Course of the Nuclear Crisis
On October 3, 2002, Assistant Secretary of State for East Asian and Pacific Affairs James Kelly became the highest-ranking U.S. official to visit Pyongyang since President George W. Bush took office. In the weeks before his visit, the U.S. intelligence community had become increasingly convinced that North Korea was pursuing a highly enriched uranium (HEU) capability in violation of the Agreed Framework. It estimated that the North had been assembling actual HEU capabilities since 2000 and that it had been "seeking centrifuge related materials in large quantities" since 2001. Kelly confronted the North Korean delegation with this estimate. Surprisingly, North Korea's First Vice Minister Kang Sok-Ju confirmed

the HEU program and justified it as a reaction to U.S. actions that had effectively nullified the Agreed Framework.

After the results of Kelly's trip to Pyongyang were made public on October 16, the confrontation escalated quickly. In November, the Korean Peninsula Energy Development Organization (KEDO) suspended heavy fuel oil shipments to the DPRK. The following month, Pyongyang announced that it would restart the operation and construction of its nuclear facilities at Yongbyon, which had been frozen since 1994. It subsequently expelled International Atomic Energy Agency (IAEA) inspectors and removed monitoring devices from its nuclear power plants, fuel and spent fuel storage areas, and reprocessing facilities. In January 2003, Pyongyang announced that it was withdrawing from the NPT. In February, the North reactivated its one functioning nuclear power plant and resumed construction work on two other unfinished— and much larger—nuclear plants.

From February to April 2003, the pace of North Korea's escalation slowed, though its rhetoric became, in many ways, more worrisome. Pyongyang did not, apparently, bring its main reprocessing facility on line, as many feared it would. It may have had second thoughts about further escalation or bowed to China's pressure, or it may have simply experienced technical difficulties. Nor did the North test medium- or long-range ballistic missiles, as it threatened and could have done. On the other hand, in late March North Korea began to take a more uncompromising stand on readmitting inspectors as part of a possible negotiated settlement.

After four months of disagreement on whether talks should be bilateral, as North Korea insisted, or multilateral, as the United States insisted, China arranged a trilateral meeting in Beijing with the United States and North Korea, something of a comedown for both countries. North Korea's pronouncements during the April 23 meeting on the reprocessing of its spent fuel rods were provocative but ambiguous. Overall, the meetings increased uncertainties about North Korea's nuclear developments and about the future direction of the dispute. North Korea and the United States presented almost mirror image positions. Washington insisted that Pyongyang had to proceed to end its HEU program and refreeze its plutonium before the United States would engage on other issues. The North advanced a concrete (if vague) proposal but insisted that it had to have security assurances from the United States before it would end its nuclear program.

For the first time, an official North Korean representative, Li Gun, deputy director general of the Foreign Ministry's American Affairs Bureau, asserted at the Beijing talks that North Korea had nuclear weapons. U.S. intelligence had previously concluded that North Korea probably had one or two weapons, so the news was not a major surprise. But the admission was, and it could have significant political and psychological impact in the region, particularly in South Korea, which had entered into a nonnuclear agreement with the North in 1992 that the DPRK has now publicly abandoned. Most important, the North Korean representative also indicated to Kelly that his country had almost completed the reprocessing of all its fuel rods, which, if true, marks a major escalation of the crisis. The intelligence community has not found evidence of such a development. It cannot be excluded that Li Gun was not telling the truth and that his remarks were designed to further pressure the United States.

Some observers believe, on the basis of additional private comments to Kelly, that the North was hinting at a new deal: American security assurances in exchange for a commitment not to test weapons and not to transfer any weapons or fissile material. Other accounts suggest that the North Korean representative implied that all of his country's nuclear programs were on the table, and that Pyongyang's new rhetoric was an attempt to push Washington to accept a deal. Responding to these developments, President Bush indicated that the United States will not be intimidated by North Korean threats.

Divergent Approaches to the North
Serious differences within the allied camp have made dealing effectively with North Korea difficult in the past, and those differences have further widened with the new nuclear crisis.

The Bush administration reversed the Clinton administration's North Korea policy, expressing skepticism about the utility of negotiated agreements with North Korea. It also adopted a skeptical attitude toward South Korea's "sunshine policy," which it felt bought off the North while getting little in return, serving only to prop up a terrible regime. A U.S. policy review, completed in June 2001, opened the door to "serious dialogue" with Pyongyang and held out the promise of further economic assistance. The bar for achieving a settlement was set high, however. It included the acceleration of IAEA safeguard compliance under the Agreed Framework; an end to North Korea's mid- and long-range missile programs; a less threatening North Korean conventional posture; improved human rights performance; and tangible steps toward economic reform. These terms were essentially presented as an all-or-nothing package, and North Korea balked at negotiations under them.

The terrorist attacks of September 11, 2001, led to a blunt presidential perspective on North Korea. In his January 2002 State of the Union address, President Bush listed North Korea as part of the "axis of evil," together with Iraq and Iran. That expression drew enormous and worried attention on both sides of the 38th parallel. Concern increased further when the U.S. Nuclear Posture Review was leaked to the press in March 2002. The review listed North Korea among the countries against which the United States might consider launching a preemptive attack with yet-to-be-designed, "usable" small nuclear weapons. Concern mounted again with the September 2002 National Security Strategy, which offered a comprehensive rationale for preemptive action against "rogue states" possessing weapons of mass destruction and identified North Korea as a prominent example.

At the same time, the State Department continued to insist that the United States would engage in talks with North Korea "any time, any place, without preconditions." In April 2002, the North finally agreed to talks. A meeting scheduled for July was called off in the wake of a gun battle between North and South Korean naval vessels and was rescheduled for early October, by which time the HEU issue had come to dominate the U.S. position.

American skepticism about dealing with North Korea did not stop ROK President Kim Dae-Jung. After a difficult year for North-South relations in 2001, he renewed his commitment to the sunshine policy in 2002. South Korean Special Envoy Lim Dong-Won traveled to Pyongyang in April, and the two sides reached agreements on opening the rail line between Seoul and Kaesong (just across the border), another reunion of separated families, and the reactivation of the Committee for Promotion of Economic Cooperation. South Korean two-way trade with the North grew by 50 percent in 2002. North Korea announced the opening of a new special industrial zone in Kaesong, and Hyundai prepared to begin work on its infrastructure. Subsequently, it became apparent that much of President Kim's engagement effort was made possible by payoffs to North Korea.

The new ROK government of Roh Moo-Hyun continues to publicly oppose U.S. efforts to pressure the North through sanctions and even to discuss the use of force. The United States, for its part, has rejected Roh's entreaties to hold bilateral talks with the North. The accidental killing of two teenage South Korean girls by U.S. servicemen in June 2002 and the clearing of the individuals involved by all-American courts martial in November—just before the ROK presidential election—have added to the tensions over policy toward the North and inflamed anti-American sentiment in the South. In a December 2002 survey by Gallup, 53 percent of South Korean respondents said they "disliked" the United States, while only 37 percent had favorable feelings (as opposed to 15 and 64 percent, respectively, in 1994). The stark decline in U.S.-ROK relations was recognized by both governments and prompted steps by both to improve the relationship. The recent meeting of the two presidents in Washington has furthered these efforts. Despite improvement in the overall relationship this year, the two states have not reached anything approaching agreement on how to deal with Pyongyang.

Japanese, Chinese, and Russian policies toward North Korea have also differed from those of the United States, though in general to lesser degrees than that of South Korea. Prime Minister Junichiro Koizumi of Japan made a determined but ultimately unsuccessful effort to normalize relations with Pyongyang last September despite tense U.S.-DPRK relations. After the October HEU revelation broke, Japan opposed sanctions but later edged closer to a tougher position on Pyongyang. Beijing has opposed sanctions and prevented condemnation of North Korea by the UN Security Council. But it has sternly warned Pyongyang in private against proceeding with nuclear threats, and there is much speculation that Beijing backed up its warnings in March with a temporary (three-day) suspension of oil deliveries. Russia is opposed to blanket sanctions against North Korea, and many Russians blame the United States for the crisis, but even Moscow has threatened to change its sanctions position if North Korea moves ahead with its nuclear weapons program.

Despite regional opposition to sanctions, the United States has been able to bring North Korea under considerable pressure. KEDO ceased oil shipments in November 2002, reducing North Korea's total oil imports by around one quarter. Despite a small American contribution, food donations to North Korea through the World Food Program have fallen. The United States has apparently persuaded South Korea, China, and Japan not to undertake major new aid or investment projects. Gradually, it won support for multilateral talks.

North Korea's Posture

North Korea's Difficult Straits

Whatever Pyongyang's intentions were when it decided at the end of 2002 to escalate rather than back down, North Korea's position over the past year has clearly become more difficult, if not precarious. Dependent on the outside world for fuel to fire its industrial plants and food to feed its people, the regime has lost much of its access to both kinds of resources. It is largely isolated diplomatically. It has been thoroughly spooked by the change from Clinton to Bush, and the chilling of relations with the United States has caused it to devote more attention and resources to its military needs. Its continuing efforts to carry out a modicum of economic reform have suffered serious setbacks. As a result of sustained economic failure, North Korea has turned itself into something of a mafia-ruled state, earning sizeable sums from narcotics and counterfeiting.

The biggest economic blow over the past year was Pyongyang's failure to obtain billions of dollars in aid from Japan by resolving the long-standing issue of abductees from Japan. Not only did Pyongyang allow abductees to return for a visit to Japan, but, to international astonishment, it apologized for the kidnappings, an implicit criticism of the late North Korean premier, Kim Il-Sung. These efforts came to naught, however, when the Japanese public was revolted by the abductees' stories and the North's nuclear gambit, forcing the Japanese government to suspend its normalization campaign.

North Korea has secured critical economic benefits from its relations with South Korea, while using its diplomacy with the South to drive a wedge between Washington and Seoul. The North has never followed through on the promise of the 2000 summit and the return visit of Kim Jong-Il to Seoul. Its actions undermined the domestic political position of South Korean President Kim Dae-Jung and have threatened to do the same to his successor, leaders who have helped with sizeable food and fertilizer deliveries when needs arose in the North. Indeed, Pyongyang has often simply watched these leaders' humiliation when they have faced strong domestic political attacks for North Korea's failure to reciprocate their largess in some fashion. The promise of another "Pyongyang spring" last year helped to produce important projects like connecting road and rail lines between North and South, but improvement in relations slowed with the failure of the North's economic reforms and the reemergence of the nuclear issue. The North has not hesitated to publicly attack the South when it disapproved of what Seoul was doing, and it has moved excruciatingly slowly on matters of great political importance to the South, such as family reunions. By and large, the North appears to have come to believe it can easily control its dealings with South Korea and further promote the anti-Americanism that has developed in the South.

Perhaps North Korea's biggest handicap in dealing with the United States is its increasing international isolation. The distancing of China—its only friend—must be of deep concern to Pyongyang. Beijing has taken a clear stand against North Korea's nuclear program, effectively putting Pyongyang on notice that it will not provide unconditional support for the regime. Japan has slowed its normalization efforts and will not commit any economic aid to the North. South Korea has been scaling back its recent bout of anti-Americanism, and in the recent summit meeting with President Bush, President Roh stated that "future inter-Korean exchanges and cooperation will be conducted in light of developments on the North Korean nuclear issue." President Roh has signaled a new appreciation for the U.S.-ROK alliance, not least by dispatching South Korean noncombat army units to assist the United States in Iraq, despite vocal North Korean and domestic criticism of the move. And even the European Union (EU) has added to the pressures by preparing a resolution criticizing North Korea's human rights record in the UN Human Rights Commission— a resolution that passed overwhelmingly. (South Korea's absence from the vote is a telling reminder of that country's unwillingness to attack North Korea's dismal human rights performance for fear of hurting its engagement efforts.)

North Korea faces yet another grim year of serious shortages of food and power. The impact of economic and diplomatic failures on the leadership is not clear. One might surmise that such a string of major failures over the past three years would have generated severe strains in the leadership. By all outward appearances, Kim Jong-Il's position seems secure. But the media's emphasis on an "imminent" American attack and the buildup of the role of the military may reflect some leadership concern regarding domestic stability. Both Russian and Chinese sources have hinted at growing dissension within the leadership. One thing remains clear: the leadership still believes it cannot open up the country and the economy for fear it will lead to the destruction of the regime.

Pyongyang's Objectives

Views of Pyongyang's intentions vary widely within and among concerned governments and among informed publics. Some have argued that Pyongyang's rhetoric, and to some extent even its behavior, suggest greater interest in working out some sort of agreement with the United States than in acquiring more nuclear weapons. Even if this is the case, however, Pyongyang may well move forward with reprocessing its spent fuel if it fails to reach an understanding with the United States. Others, however, believe that North Korea is determined to obtain a substantial nuclear weapons capability as the only serious deterrent against a U.S. attack. If that is true, then North Korea's interest in working out a nuclear agreement is spurious and presumably designed to generate international restraint on the United States and secure renewed foreign aid, as it continues all the while its nuclear efforts.

There are major uncertainties in any assessment of North Korea's intentions, and prudence is in order in evaluating its behavior. North Korean politics and decision-making are opaque. Official statements are frequently vague or contradictory. Even when public pronouncements are clear, it is difficult to discern what is real and what is tactical. Pyongyang's penchant for brinksmanship and threats further undermine efforts to understand the North. The Task Force's assessment of North Korea's position considers Pyongyang's words and actions, viewed in the context of the "normal" background noise—i.e., the government's historical behavior. This assessment is not immune from the uncertainties mentioned above.

The Task Force believes that Pyongyang's attitude has hardened over time, especially since February of this year. Prior to that time, North Korea showed strong interest in a negotiated settlement, although it was not clear on what terms. Since then, continuing appeals for negotiations have been mixed with an increasing number of statements defending its right to produce nuclear weapons. North Korea may or may not still be open to serious negotiations.

Negotiations?

On October 25, 2002, nine days after the United States announced the results of the Kelly-Kang meetings, North Korea declared that it would "be ready to seek a negotiated settlement" in which it would "clear U.S. security concerns" if the United States was willing to "assure us of nonaggression." Distrustful that the United States would not live up to its promises, Pyongyang has also at times insisted that assurances from the executive branch would not be enough; a formal nonaggression treaty must be ratified by Congress. North Korea has also declared that it wants assurances that the United States will not block economic aid or whatever economic deals Pyongyang makes with other states.

Following the Israeli, Pakistani, or Indian models, one would expect that if North Korea had been sprinting toward a full-scale nuclear weapons program, it would have done so as quietly as possible. This was, in fact, how North Korea pursued its HEU program. Yet between last October and this February—and arguably since then—North Korea has openly telegraphed its escalatory moves, including, for example, its moves to eject IAEA inspectors from the country and restart its nuclear facilities. This pattern is consistent with an effort to bring the United States to the bargaining table, though it is not necessarily incompatible with a decision to build nuclear weapons. The interception of an American reconnaissance aircraft over international waters on March 2 and the test firing of Silkworm antiship missiles, including one the day before President Roh's inauguration, also appeared designed to put further pressure on the United States for a settlement. (In the latter case, North Korea's selection of a short-range missile not covered under its self-imposed moratorium on missile testing indicates some careful weighing of its efforts.)

Pyongyang's apparent desire for security assurances is consistent with its past behavior and rhetoric. In negotiating the Agreed Framework, much of the North's bargaining centered on gaining provisions for lifting sanctions, normalization of relations, and formal assurances of nonuse of nuclear weapons against it. Pyongyang has frequently complained—with some reason—that the United States was not complying fully with those provisions. The United States lifted some but not all sanctions in 1999, has not normalized relations, and did not provide unequivocal assurances on the issue of nuclear attack. (The United States notes that North Korean red tape contributed to delays in building the reactors that the Agreed Framework promised for electrical power and that the North took a full year to dispatch a high-level delegation to discuss normalization-related issues toward the end of the Clinton administration.) In the months prior to October 2002, the North expressed alarm over its inclusion in the "axis of evil" and designation as a possible target for preemptive attack. By all appearances, Pyongyang is genuinely concerned about its external security. The decisive U.S. victory in Iraq must have made this concern even more acute. North Korean leaders might well believe that deterrence is better accomplished through nuclear weapons than endless negotiations.

The North's pursuit of an HEU program predated President Bush and therefore cannot be explained by any action of his administration. But the North's acquisition of actual capabilities (as opposed to research) does not appear to have predated North Korea's more general complaints about U.S. behavior. North Korea complained repeatedly during negotiations with the Clinton administration in 1998 and 1999 that the United States was violating the Agreed Framework by failing to move forward on normalization. It is entirely possible that Pyongyang's HEU program followed its own schedule and logic, and was unrelated to U.S. actions. But the apparent timing of key events also makes it possible that the speed at which the North pursued its HEU program, as well as Pyongyang's changing negotiating position since October 2002, may be partly explained by its increasing fear of the United States.

Most people who have been in direct contact with the North have come away with the impression that it is deeply concerned about its security and eager to secure an agreement with the United States. Chinese, Russian, and South Korean interlocutors have all emphasized this impression, as did Bill Richardson, former U.S. ambassador to the United Nations, who met with North Korean officials in January. Maurice Strong, acting as a UN envoy to North Korea in March, summarized his meeting: "A security guarantee is what they want. It is the absolute conviction of [North Korea] that they are under threat." Even before March, it was unclear whether Pyongyang would have agreed to terms that could have been accepted by the United States. But its eagerness to negotiate was in little doubt.

Pyongyang will expect compensation for assets surrendered, destroyed, or frozen—costs the United States would probably expect its allies to pay. An even greater incentive for the North to reach a settlement is the potential for renewed "engagement" with South Korea, China, Japan, and Russia and the aid and investment that might follow in the wake of an agreement. From the U.S. and allied perspective, the possibility that an end to North Korea's isolation might be accompanied by at least rudimentary efforts at economic reform—as was the case before October 2002, despite some risk to the regime—provides some degree of parallel incentive, though any firm expectations on this point would be sanguine at best.

A Tougher Stance?
North Korea's actions and its public pronouncements since February and especially since late March suggest its position may be changing or may have already changed.

There are indications that the influence of the North Korean military, already much increased since the gradual institutional decline of the Workers' Party during the 1980s and 1990s, has been further strengthened. On March 21, 2003, the *Nodong Sinmun* (Worker's Party Newspaper) carried a two-page special article extolling the country's "military-first ideology" and emphasizing that economic growth and even the welfare of the working classes must take a back seat to strengthening the military. Shortly thereafter, the North Korean Supreme People's Assembly passed a military service law that included provisions for the conscription of party and government officials who had been exempted from earlier service by virtue of their official posts.

Pyongyang's public statements on the nuclear issue have changed noticeably. On April 10, 2003, the North Korean media suggested that Iraq's "fatal mistake" had been to admit weapons inspectors into the country and suggested, "The only way of averting a war is to increase one's own just self-defense means." During the Beijing meetings, North Korean officials went further, abandoning the pretext that the North's development of nuclear capabilities was purely peaceful and, on the contrary, stating the need for a "powerful physical deterrent force."

It is possible that the North Korean leadership has already decided to move ahead with the further development of nuclear capabilities. Nevertheless, despite a general toughening of rhetoric and action, the signals from North Korea continue to be mixed. During the April meetings in Beijing, Pyongyang tabled a proposal for a comprehensive settlement, and, although the terms were clearly unacceptable to the United States, it is possible that it may, if probed, prove flexible. North Korea's media has occasionally continued to repeat the argument that negotiations are the only peaceful solution to the impasse. In late May 2003, North Korean officials again reportedly told a visiting congressional delegation they were willing to trade their nuclear weapons programs for security assurances and other concessions from the United States. Despite the military's bureaucratic power, Kim Jong-Il apparently continues to wield exceptional power and can make decisive decisions.

It is difficult to predict how Pyongyang's weakened economic and diplomatic state—and the aftereffects of America's victory in Iraq—will affect its future negotiating position. North Korea has been through difficult times for many years. Conceivably, present economic circumstances are sufficiently more difficult to cause the North to rethink its current posture and make concessions in hopes of resolving the impasse. On the other hand, isolation, economic malaise, and increased fears of U.S. attack could further empower the military and validate a continued tough line. Recent signs are not encouraging.

THE U.S. GOVERNMENT'S POSTURE

The Bush administration has, from its inception, been divided over policy toward North Korea. One group favored continuing engagement but on different terms from those the Clinton administration had pursued. These officials favored a settlement that would address wider concerns including conventional forces and tougher verification, and they were prepared to offer more in the way of economic assistance in exchange for reforms. A second group held that the Agreed Framework was a disaster, that the North Korean regime was a multifaceted threat both regionally and globally, and that any agreement with such a regime would be unenforceable. The members of this group believed that regime change should be the goal of U.S. policy. Only in this way could real stability on the peninsula be achieved, though the group also recognized the difficulties involved in pursuing any military action against North Korean nuclear facilities. Its members also believed that Kim Dae-Jung's engagement policy only served to help the North Korean regime survive and avoid change.

The division in the administration continues. For the moment, the debate has been focused on whether North Korea must provide tangible evidence that its nuclear program has stopped before any negotiations begin, or whether the United States should be willing to negotiate a relatively comprehensive tough package deal. The Beijing talks did not resolve this debate, since those meetings were not defined as negotiations but rather as an opportunity for each side to lay out its position. Whatever the debate, and even if another round of talks is convened, there are no signs that the president has decided to engage in serious negotiations.

Since January 2003, the United States has consistently emphasized several themes: (1) the North Korean nuclear weapons program is a regional problem and requires a multilateral, not simply a bilateral, forum for any talks with North Korea; (2) confidence that a peaceful solution to the nuclear problem can be achieved while attempting to downplay the urgency of the situation; (3) a refusal to "reward bad behavior"; and (4) a diplomatic emphasis on gaining China's support and cooperation. The talks in Beijing indicate some compromise on the administration's multilateral emphasis and a reinforcement of China's role. At the same time, recent diplomacy with Japan and other states aimed at coordinating the interdiction of illegal exports and illegal shipping indicates an effort to expand the economic pressure on North Korea.

Multilateralism

Administration officials have provided four rationales for their insistence on multilateral negotiations. First, since the North Korean nuclear weapons program affects the security of all states in the region—as well as, potentially, other regions of the world—the regional powers must all have a voice in, and take responsibility for, resolving this issue. Second, since none of North Korea's neighbors wants the North to acquire nuclear weapons, a multilateral forum would allow these states to exert additional pressure on the North to abandon its program. Third, having participated in negotiations, America's partners would have an obligation to assist in the enforcement of any agreements. Finally, the multilateral approach could get around the constraint created by congressional unwillingness to provide funds for North Korea.

Noncrisis Rhetoric

U.S. policymakers have sought since October to project confidence in an eventual peaceful resolution and have assiduously avoided describing the situation as a crisis. Secretary of State Colin Powell has repeatedly stated that there is time for diplomacy to work, and officials from President Bush on down have sought to assure North Korea that the United States has no plans to invade it. This posture avoided complicating the diplomatic and military preparations for the war in Iraq and endangering domestic public support for the administration. It has also avoided giving North Korea leverage by suggesting the United States was impatient for a settlement. But how the administration expects diplomacy to work and a peaceful settlement to emerge without some form of negotiations is not clear.

No Rewards for Bad Behavior

A third theme, one that predates the current nuclear standoff, is an unwillingness to "reward bad behavior" or allow North Korea to "retail the threat"—i.e., generate a variety of threats in order to gain a never-ending string of concessions or get paid twice for removing a single threat. The administration has not articulated what kind of a deal it might either present or accept if and when its preferred multilateral negotiations occur, but its fear of buying off threats retail would seem to require a comprehensive arrangement. Paradoxically, however, the same underlying fear of "rewarding bad behavior" may make any deal politically difficult for the administration.

Sinocentric Diplomacy

The United States has heavily emphasized bilateral diplomacy with China to persuade Beijing to support pressure against the North. Secretary of State Powell, Deputy Secretary of State Richard Armitage, Assistant Secretary of State Kelly, and Under Secretary of State John Bolton have all led separate delegations to Beijing. The administration believes that China has the most clout with North Korea and should be prepared to use it to stop Pyongyang's nuclear weapons program. China has a major interest in preventing a North Korean nuclear weapons program that might spur the nuclearization of Japan or South Korea. Because China does not want a war on its border, it should do everything possible to avoid the emergence of circumstances under which the United States might attack North Korean nuclear facilities. China appears to have come some distance toward the U.S. position, though Beijing still believes that any settlement must be negotiated directly between Washington and Pyongyang.

The most difficult questions about U.S. policy revolve around its making: Can a consensus be established within the Bush administration on policy toward North Korea? Will the president simply continue to refuse to deal with North Korea? Or will he intervene decisively to establish a new policy course? Can the United States accept an agreement with North Korea that does not involve the suicide of the Pyongyang regime? The recent impasse with North

Korea over the forum for talks left differences within the administration unresolved but hidden by the common demand for multilateralism.

THE ROK AND OTHER REGIONAL STATES

In contrast to the United States, key regional states—Japan, South Korea, China, and Russia—have felt a sense of urgency in seeking ways to defuse the crisis. Although they supported the decision to proceed with the Beijing meeting, Japan and South Korea have expressed some consternation at being left out of the first round of talks in China. But all three states have persistently—both before and since those talks—encouraged the United States to engage North Korea in direct negotiations. Despite the commonalities, however, significant differences exist among the policies favored by these states. Some current stances could, however, be altered by events or heavy American pressure.

Republic of Korea
South Korea had a presidential election in December 2002, but the transition from Kim Dae-Jung to Roh Moo-Hyun has not so far led to fundamental changes in the country's engagement policy. Despite increasing domestic criticism of Kim's management of policy toward North Korea and charges that he purchased the 2000 summit meeting, South Korea's new government has been persistent in trying to maintain its dealings with the North, even in the face of rebuffs from Pyongyang and despite the growing nuclear imbroglio.

After the results of Kelly's October 2002 meetings in Pyongyang became public, South Korea announced an acceleration of economic cooperation with the North, including the opening of a new industrial park in the North Korean city of Kaesong. Explaining the need for engagement, President Kim said, "Pressure and isolation have never been successful with Communist countries." Shortly after his election, President-elect Roh said that even talk about military action was unacceptable. He set off alarm bells in Washington by suggesting that Seoul could "mediate" the conflict between Pyongyang and Washington.

With widely divergent views of the North Korean problem, officials in Washington and Seoul looked for ways to close the gap— or at least shore up the alliance in general terms. In November 2002, Seoul agreed to drop its objections to the suspension of KEDO's heavy fuel oil shipments. After casting doubt on the need for U.S. troops on the peninsula, Roh made the first visit ever by a president-elect to the Republic of Korea-U.S. Combined Forces Command in January and stated bluntly that the alliance "has been, is, and will be important." Although Defense Secretary Donald Rumsfeld's expression of interest in possibly removing and relocating ground forces reminded Koreans that they had better be careful what they wished for, the Pentagon has been reassuring South Korea that it will not take military action without consulting Seoul. The Pentagon also appears intent on resolving long-festering base issues in South Korea. In June 2003, the United States and the ROK announced a plan to consolidate U.S. forces and later pull U.S. troops stationed close to the Demilitarized Zone to positions south of Seoul and also for units to vacate the Yongsan base inside the capital.

Since October 2002, South Korea has consistently called for the United States and North Korea to engage in direct talks. Although the South Korean popular media has shown disappointment at Seoul's exclusion from the first round of talks with North Korea in April, Roh's government has expressed satisfaction that it would be involved at the end of the day. Resolving the nuclear crisis, Roh said, should take precedence over South Korean participation in any particular round. This is especially true, he said, given the damage that the continuing crisis is doing to the South Korean economy, an increasingly important consideration in the government's decision-making.

It is not surprising that substantial policy differences persist between the two governments. The United States would like to see the North Korean regime disappear; the ROK wants to keep it alive, at least until the North's economic situation is improved and unification can take place on less financially costly terms. The sense of shared danger from the North has diminished among many South Koreans, particularly younger ones, who have no memory of the Korean War. Given the disparity between the two Koreas, many perceive the North as more of a charity case than a threat to their survival. They complain about a lack of American respect for Korean views. They consider threats to destroy North Korean nuclear facilities a danger to their lives and fantastic material achievements and far more costly than living with a nuclearized North Korea. The North has long sold deadly materials to "bad" states, and the United States greatly fears it will likely continue to do so with fissile materials. For South Koreans, however, this fear rates far below other concerns. Whether these differences can be bridged is uncertain, given the parties' different geopolitical circumstances. President Roh's visit to Washington was designed to deepen the sense of cooperation. Although the two governments avoided a diplomatic disaster like Kim Dae-Jung's trip to Washington in 2001, it ultimately proved difficult to conceal the major policy differences lying just below the surface.

China
The intensive U.S. lobbying of China has paid dividends, although serious differences on Korean policy remain. Beijing has continued to loudly affirm the desirability of a nonnuclear peninsula, much to the annoyance of Pyongyang. It reportedly was distressed over North Korea's behavior at the April trilateral meeting in Beijing. But China has preferred quiet, if sometimes tough, persuasion over internationally imposed sanctions. Beijing voted within the IAEA to refer North Korea's withdrawal to the UN Security Council for deliberation but blocked efforts in the Security Council to criticize Pyongyang or impose sanctions. It wants Washington to negotiate with Pyongyang seriously and directly.

China prefers low-profile diplomacy, and the role the United States has bestowed on Beijing during the current crisis is not necessarily a welcome one. But China has a great interest in the Korean Peninsula, one that has changed over the years. Its primary focus had been North Korea. To the extent that this is still true, its interests in the North are now strategic and no longer ideological.

Beijing has little love for Pyongyang. It is unhappy at the flow of North Korean refugees, and it is afraid that a North Korean collapse would bring a flood of Koreans to China. It is probably more afraid that North Korea's nuclear program will unleash a war on the peninsula or that the North's acquisition of a significant nuclear weapons stockpile could, as noted earlier, lead South Korea and Japan to seek their own nuclear deterrents. China has played host to Kim Jong-Il and invited him to Shanghai in hopes of persuading North Korea to reform its economy. (The North went a little way toward reform but botched the effort.) China has continued to finance North Korea's trade deficits and supplies between 70 and 90 percent of its oil and a considerable portion of its food imports.

While its affection for the North dwindles, China's interest in South Korea has risen sharply. China has become the ROK's largest trading partner, and investment and economic ties between the two have grown exponentially. Favorable popular sentiment toward China has risen significantly in South Korea, and there are increasing cultural and other exchanges between the two nations. Both countries have come to share the same approach to dealing with the North, including the nuclear issue. Similarly, the vast expansion of China's ties with the United States and its interest in deepening them has made the neuralgic Korean issue a subject of common concern. China's desire to avoid a U.S. attack on North Korea's nuclear facilities has given Washington significant leverage with Beijing.

China has undertaken intensive bilateral discussions with the North. According to one report, Chinese officials have met with North Korean counterparts 60 times to discuss the nuclear issue. In early March 2003, the Chinese government reportedly formed a Leading Group on the North Korean Crisis (LGNKC), headed by Hu Jintao and designed both to coordinate policy and to improve intelligence collection and analysis on North Korea's nuclear program. Chinese envoys have reportedly warned Kim Jong-Il that any attack against the United States, U.S. forces, or U.S. allies in the region is likely to bring an overwhelming U.S. response and that China will not come to Pyongyang's assistance. Perhaps most intriguing of all, there are reports that the oil pipeline from China to North Korea experienced "technical difficulties" and was shut down for three days some time during March—an event that surely sent a powerful signal to Pyongyang. China's relations with North Korea are clearly troubled.

Japan

Tokyo has fallen into line with a tougher U.S. approach to North Korea after efforts to finally normalize relations with Pyongyang failed late in 2002 and the nuclear issue reared its head. It is unclear, however, how far Japan will go in support of its American ally in reversing North Korean nuclear efforts.

Unlike South Korea, Japan has few interests in the North. Moreover, the Japanese public is deeply suspicious of the North, a feeling heightened by the recent experience of the return of the abductees. The government is mostly concerned about the North Korean nuclear program and Pyongyang's ability to marry a nuclear capability to missiles. North Korea has some 100 Nodong missiles that could be fired against Japan. But while Tokyo fears further North Korean nuclear and missile development, it also worries that a U.S. attack designed to destroy North Korean nuclear facilities would be met with a missile attack on Japan. Japan's interest in missile defense has increased, and it has launched its first intelligence satellites to watch North Korean missile efforts.

Japan has moved carefully on the nuclear issue. It initially joined South Korea in resisting U.S. calls to suspend KEDO's heavy fuel oil shipments in November, although both ultimately relented. Japan also joined South Korea in appealing for a peaceful resolution to outstanding problems. It encouraged the United States to negotiate directly with North Korea. Recently, however, Japan's position has hardened. Although Tokyo still favors negotiations, when it looked as if the United States would seek sanctions against the North, reports suggested that the Japanese government would likely support that action. Japan's potential leverage with the North is less than that of either China or South Korea, but possible sanctions could include a cutoff of funding for KEDO, a ban on remittances by North Koreans living in Japan to Pyongyang, and trade sanctions.

Japan's actual commitment to sanctions remains somewhat ambiguous. In February 2003, senior U.S. officials said that planning for sanctions against North Korea included cutting off remittances from Japan. As soon as the reports appeared, however, Chief Cabinet Secretary Yasuo Fukuda said, "Right now, we are not considering sanctions, nor have there been any discussions [about them]." Tokyo has slowed the flow of remittances from Japan to North Korea. It has also imposed an inspection regime on North Korean ships docking in Japanese ports, discouraging illegal activities by their crews and further slowing the flow of hard currency to the North. But comprehensive sanctions would depend on the passage of a UN resolution or, at a minimum, on the consensus of all relevant states. Japan is opposed to the use of force against North Korean nuclear facilities but appears closer to joining in ratcheting up the pressure on North Korea.

Japan has been cautious about its own military posture. Defense Agency Chief Shigeru Ishiba stated in January 2003 that Japan has the right to launch preemptive attacks on missile sites preparing to launch. Even then, however, he softened his statement by admitting that Japan does not have the capability to actually execute such a mission. And in early March, he stepped back further, saying that Japan would not use its own forces against the North but would rely on U.S. forces to strike back in the event of hostilities. In any case, it remains clear that Japan has sought to strengthen its military alliance with the United States since October. Notable in this regard was Prime Minister Koizumi's strong statement of support for the war in Iraq and his efforts to clear legal obstacles to the dispatch of Ground Self-Defense Forces support units to assist in the reconstruction effort after the war. But while Tokyo has strengthened its military ties with Washington, it continues to urge the United States to enter "concrete" negotiations with North Korea on resolving the nuclear issue peacefully.

Russia

Moscow largely blamed the United States for causing the crisis last October, and as recently as April 9 Russia teamed up with China to block a UN Security Council presidential statement condemning North Korea's withdrawal from the NPT. Russia has been even firmer in opposing any discussion of sanctions within the United Nations.

But Moscow has recognized its own interests in maintaining a nonnuclear peninsula, and it has leaned on North Korea to halt its nuclear weapons program. After North Korea announced its withdrawal from the NPT on January 10, the Russian Foreign Ministry said the statement had "aroused deep concern" in Moscow and expressed "the hope that Pyongyang will listen to the unanimous opinion of the world community" by coming into compliance with its international obligations. Shortly thereafter, Russian Deputy Foreign Minister Alexander Losyukov traveled to Pyongyang to discuss a package deal that, according to Russian sources, had been discussed with officials from the United States and other concerned states. Losyukov suggested that one or more external parties, either individually or collectively under UN leadership, could monitor and guarantee an agreement between the United States and North Korea.

Although Russia's January attempt to play the role of peacemaker failed, Moscow remains a potentially important part of a negotiated solution. Plans to extend the Siberian railroad through North Korea to the South were well advanced before last October. The realization of this link has been indefinitely delayed by the current crisis, but the prospect of its completion is important to Moscow and provides a positive incentive for North Korea to settle with the international community. In late March, Ra Jong-Yil, South Korea's national security adviser, traveled to Moscow and proposed that Russia could, as part of a final settlement, also supply natural gas to North Korea. (Presumably, South Korea would offset part or all of the cost.)

In addition to its possible role in providing positive incentives to the North, Russia has also suggested a greater willingness to consider sanctions. On April 11, 2003, two days after Russia helped block forceful action by the United Nations, Losyukov clarified Moscow's position, saying, "We will oppose this approach [sanctions] as long as our North Korean colleagues maintain common sense. ... But Russia will have to seriously consider its position as the appearance in North Korea of nuclear weapons and the possibility of its using them close to our borders goes categorically against the national interests of Russia." Russia's voice on North Korea remains more mixed than Losyukov's statement would suggest, but Moscow is positioned to play a positive role in any multilateral resolution of the crisis.

FORMULATING A POLICY TOWARD NORTH KOREA

The Korean problem gets increasingly dangerous because of the decrepit nature of the North Korean state and its lack of options. Its chances of turning into a more normal state are slim, and Pyongyang must be prevented from doing great damage during its remaining days. The North is showing itself to be mendacious and increasingly a loose cannon, but we cannot count on a policy of isolation to end its efforts to develop weapons of mass destruction (WMD). Miscalculation usually accompanies isolation. Nor can the United States count on China, however helpful to date, to be its silver bullet to resolve the nuclear problem peacefully. The United States cannot tarry much longer in coming up with a coherent policy. If the issue is not resolved soon, the United States could even find itself learning to live with a North Korea with more nuclear weapons.

The quick collapse of the North Korean regime is an objective on which many Americans can agree. But the strategies designed to achieve that objective are ones that South Korea and other regional states strongly oppose because, among other things, those strategies carry an inherent risk of war. The pursuit of regime change would require enormous American pressure on U.S. partners to participate in an effort that might, in any case, fail. Even in the highly unlikely event other states were to sign on, a policy of isolation and strangulation would still take considerable time, yield its own set of uncertainties, and prevent the United States from dealing effectively with the nuclear issue—unless the United States were to resign itself to simply live with whatever nuclear capability the North decides to pursue. The Task Force, therefore, does not believe this approach is an acceptable policy in the short term, although we do not preclude regime change as an outcome of the present crisis.

The Task Force argues that the United States has a choice of two broad approaches to the nuclear crisis:

- A serious effort to reach a negotiated settlement to satisfy basic concerns of both sides. Such a settlement would preferably be pursued preferably multilaterally or possibly bilaterally— or in both ways. Negotiations could focus on a broad settlement or a narrow settlement, although so far the North has only been interested in the latter. Agreement would have to involve tradeoffs by each party.

- Forceful measures to push the DPRK to give up its nuclear capabilities. Such measures could range from isolation to sanctions to the use of force. Sanctions could be imposed on remittances, North Korean arms sales, and general trade. Military force could include a naval blockade to interdict fissile materials, arms exports, drugs, and counterfeit currency, as well as air strikes designed to destroy known critical nuclear facilities. This approach would over time effectively turn into a strategy of regime change.

Problems To Be Resolved in Reaching a Strategy
Given the deep interest of America's principal allies and friends in stability on the Korean Peninsula, any serious strategy should have the agreement of China, Japan, South Korea, and Russia. Achieving an agreement, we believe, will require that the United States make a good-faith effort at negotiating a settlement with North Korea before it pursues tougher options with U.S. allies. But the United States must not allow its friends to relax while it does all the heavy lifting. The United States must make clear to its region-

al partners that they have many responsibilities on this issue. This strategy must also have an agreed-upon fallback option if negotiations do not produce results. The problem is further complicated by timing considerations—the uncertainty as to when North Korea can or will move to produce more nuclear weapons material.

The Question of Unity

Whatever the niceties of diplomatic rhetoric, the gulf between the United States and its regional partners on the nuclear issue has had governments working at cross-purposes. The ROK, under Kim and now under Roh, wants to continue its policy of engagement, refuses to support confrontational policies, and strongly opposes a resort to force. Military strikes designed to destroy North Korean nuclear facilities would be a unilateral U.S. effort that, even if they were successful and did not lead to a general war, would have grave implications for the U.S.-ROK alliance. Japan has maintained a tougher line toward the North than the ROK and seems ready, if necessary, to go down the sanctions route. It has already taken steps to restrict remittances to North Korea from Koreans in Japan. But Japan, like South Korea, is opposed to the use of force to destroy North Korea's nuclear facilities. China's attitude toward the North has been changing, but it is not clear whether China would join in a united sanctions effort if North Korea continues to pursue its WMD program. In the past, China has been willing to threaten North Korea with reduced assistance, but it has also been committed to providing life support to North Korea. No sanctions regime could work without China's participation.

The Question of Venue

The Bush administration has been attacked for refusing to engage in serious bilateral discussions, as the North insists, and for insisting on a multilateral forum to deal with the nuclear issue. It has also been accused domestically of allowing a dangerous situation to drift while holding out for that multilateral forum. The fact is that any approach to North Korea must have both a bilateral and a multilateral aspect, and each can work to reinforce the other. Only the United States can effectively handle the technical nuclear negotiation, and only the United States has the capability to destroy North Korean facilities. At the same time, however, the other regional countries have a profound interest in stopping North Korea's nuclear program, and the burden should not be only on the United States. Moreover, it is clear that for political reasons the United States will not provide large-scale assistance other than food to North Korea. Any arrangement with North Korea thus should have a multilateral dimension covering issues ranging from economic assistance to a multilateral requirement for security on the peninsula and an end to the Korean War. The multilateral approach also brings greater pressure to bear on Pyongyang, particularly from China, and gives the countries involved a stake in the overall process and its outcome. It may also facilitate subsequent action in the United Nations should bilateral negotiations falter.

There are a number of potential fora for multilateral talks. A trilateral forum including China, the United States, and North Korea has already been used. The existing but dormant four-power talks would add South Korea to the mix. A six-party forum is better because, by adding Russia and Japan, it includes all of the countries with a deep interest in the nuclear issue. The United Nations is also a possible venue. Four-power talks may be more acceptable to the North because the forum already exists. The difficulty, of course, has been Pyongyang's refusal to accept a multilateral forum and its insistence on bilateral negotiations with the United States. Given that both the Chinese and the North Koreans have said that China's role in the recently completed Beijing talks was more that of host than participant, the impasse has not been entirely broken. In part, the question of forum depends on how much time governments deem is available before North Korean developments preclude any negotiating forum.

The question of available time is critical but difficult to assess, and in some respects the answers appear confused. Originally, it was argued that North Korea could start reprocessing its spent fuel within several months and produce half a dozen weapons six months later. Now the issue is less clear. There appears to be a loss of confidence in the certainty of U.S. intelligence. If the U.S. intelligence community is correct that North Korea is not reprocessing—a judgment Pyongyang has put in doubt—either North Korea has been experiencing difficulties reprocessing, or it has decided not to move forward because of Chinese pressures or an interest in negotiating with the United States. The issue of time is also uncertain in the case of North Korea's HEU program. The U.S. government initially asserted that it would take almost two years for the program to start producing fissile material. More recently, the government reduced the time to "a matter of months," now explained to mean perhaps by the end of this year. The Task Force does not have enough information to make a judgment on this point.

RECOMMENDATIONS

1. *Mending the U.S.-ROK alliance.* The first order of business is to restore greater harmony to U.S.-ROK relations. Both countries recognize the need for unity and have done much to reduce abrasions. Achieving unity, however, will not be easy, given the inexperience of the new South Korean administration and its consuming fear of violence on the peninsula and considering the evolving views of the South Korean people. Most important, the vitality of the alliance depends on an agreed-upon approach to North Korea. President Roh's visit to Washington in May 2003 furthered the effort to reduce differences. Conceivably, unity could best be elaborated and promoted through a special high-level bilateral body to frame both short- and long-term goals for the Korean Peninsula. Whether or not such a group is established, the following elements should be part of an effort to revitalize the bilateral relationship:

- Until the nuclear crisis is resolved, the United States and South Korea should minimize public differences on North Korean policy as well as on technical military issues related to the U.S. troop presence in South Korea.

- The United States needs to find ways to reduce the abrasions generated by the Status of Forces Agreement (SOFA), a particularly thorny issue. Conceivably, joint U.S.-ROK military courts might be a useful avenue to explore. Creative solutions to this major public relations problem must be found, lest another incident threaten the health of the alliance.

- The two nations must strengthen the public side of the alliance, particularly with respect to the South Korean people. The responsibility here lies mostly with the ROK government, which must make clear to its public the importance of the bilateral alliance.

- The United States and South Korea need to discuss the long-term presence—if any—of U.S. forces in the ROK. The long-held notion that the South Koreans want U.S. forces there permanently seems out of date. The U.S. headquarters at Yongsan will be moved. Meanwhile, both countries have recently agreed to concentrate the U.S. force presence in a small number of locations and pull the 2nd Infantry Division south of Seoul. Any actual reductions in troop strengths or redeployments within South Korea should, however, be delayed until after the nuclear crisis is resolved.

- Some issues, especially the more technical ones, are being addressed by a joint team from the U.S. State and Defense Departments and their South Korean counterparts. Much progress has reportedly been made on the SOFA issue. We applaud these efforts and hope that high-level diplomatic efforts support unity of purpose in broad political terms as well as on narrower points of alliance design.

2. *High-level policy coordinator for Korea.* Given the importance and diplomatic complexity of Korean issues, there is a clear need for a distinguished full-time, high-level coordinator. Such a coordinator could help to resolve the deep divisions within the administration on the North Korean nuclear issue. The Task Force recommended a similar arrangement to the Clinton admin-

istration at a time when the executive and legislative branches were virtually at war over Korea policy.

The coordinator should be responsible for helping to determine and coordinate policy within the administration, developing a common strategy with friends and allies, and, at the appropriate time, leading negotiations with senior North Korean leaders. To the extent that there are realistic prospects for achieving a negotiated, verifiable end to North Korea's nuclear and missile programs, those prospects rest on direct negotiations at the highest levels in Korea and would require the involvement of a very senior official.

3. *Reaching an agreed strategy to deal with the North.* Recognizing the difficulties of bringing South Korea and other U.S. friends and allies on board for a common strategy, the Task Force proposes the following guidelines for reaching a multilateral/bilateral one:

- The allied side will proceed on a multilateral/bilateral basis.

- The United States will commit publicly to negotiate in any forum—the United Nations, trilateral talks, the four- or six-power group—an agreement with North Korea that provides for an end to its nuclear program with effective verification in exchange for security assurances and diplomatic recognition. Should North Korea show interest in wider security arrangements, the United States would be prepared to engage in such a negotiating effort while consulting closely with South Korea and Japan.

- On the basis of the above recommendations, the ROK will manage its bilateral dealings with North Korea at a pace consistent with U.S.-North Korean negotiations.

- The wider multilateral group will negotiate regional security guarantees with the relevant parties, including a commitment to a nonnuclear Korea, aid and other assistance to the North Korean economy, and a variety of conditions related to that aid.

- The wider regional group must accept greater responsibility for stopping the North Korean nuclear weapons program. No agreements with North Korea will be reached without South

Korea, Japan, and China committing themselves beforehand to isolating and imposing sanctions on North Korea if it refuses to end its nuclear program. Such a commitment may not actually bind U.S. allies, but it would serve to put pressure on them to maintain consistent behavior. If negotiations prove the North intransigent, U.S. partners must be held accountable for further action.

4. *The bilateral negotiation.* There should be no illusions; reaching a negotiated settlement to eliminate North Korea's nuclear program, one that adequately addresses U.S. verification concerns, will be difficult, if not impossible. The proposed settlement, given the North's covert HEU program, will require more from North Korea than the Agreed Framework did. Given the experience of the Agreed Framework, the requirements of any new agreement should be front-loaded as much as is feasible and clear benchmarks should be established. Realistically, benchmarks cannot be one-sided, requiring North Korea (or the United States) to accomplish all its tasks first but rather, to the extent possible, should require alternating sets of actions that reassure each side that its concerns are being and will continue to be met.

After resisting comprehensive negotiations for years, Pyongyang now at least claims to embrace the idea of settling nuclear and missile issues together, a combination that would be necessary to gain full Japanese support for an agreement and that, in any case, should be sought by the United States. Washington, in turn, should address North Korean security concerns and be prepared to clear external foreign obstacles to North Korea's domestic economic reform.

Any agreement should require certain early actions by North Korea. The North must reseal its spent nuclear fuel and begin transferring it out of the country on a fixed timetable. This requirement will now have to include the spent fuel from the North's current operation of the five-megawatt experimental reactor at Yongbyon. It also must include any plutonium North Korea may already have separated from its spent fuel. Pyongyang must rejoin the NPT and allow IAEA inspectors to verify the freeze on its nuclear program and complete safeguard inspections.

The United States should also make every effort to dismantle North Korea's gas-graphite reactors, including those under construction. The United States and its partners should be prepared to provide replacement conventional plants as the nuclear reactors are destroyed. The North must also account for material associated with the secret HEU program and allow a regime of adequate verification to ensure that no such program exists in the future. This is a stiff set of demands for a secretive state like North Korea to accept.

The United States should be prepared to provide formal written assurances that it will not launch any kind of attack on the North while the negotiations are proceeding. It should commit to more open-ended security assurances once the IAEA has finished its initial round of inspections, though the terms of any agreement should make U.S. assurances conditional on continued compliance with IAEA safeguards. The United States should establish a timetable for the early establishment of diplomatic relations, perhaps in conjunction with the phased removal of spent fuel from the North. The allies will have to provide some kind of compensation for the early dismantling of the North's gas-graphite nuclear reactors and for the North's surrender of its missile program. The United States must recognize that North Korea will not easily agree to replace the light-water reactors (LWRs).

This agreement hardly rewards "bad behavior." On the contrary, it would punish past and present shortcomings. The North, recognizing that its HEU program violated the Agreed Framework, will have to accept a more intrusive inspection regime and will not be trusted with LWRs. The United States will have to address North Korean perceptions that the United States failed to live up to its agreements on normalization and the lifting of economic sanctions by fixing a timetable for the resolution of those issues. The compensation for the North's lost electrical capacity is also not a free gift or a reward for threat—the North's completed and partially completed nuclear facilities would be destroyed and its considerable investment in nuclear technology lost.

5. *Redouble efforts with China to pressure North Korea.* China's status as North Korea's largest aid donor and its unique diplomatic relationship with the North give it a critical role in any effort to resolve the nuclear issue peacefully. China has to take greater responsibility for convincing North Korea to stop its nuclear program. The administration has been correct to emphasize China in its North Korean diplomacy and should intensify its efforts to gain Beijing's full cooperation in pressuring the North. Any negotiations with North Korea must have China's support, and implementation of any agreement must have China's full participation. Given that Beijing may have to pay monetary and political costs if North Korea collapses and that further pressure from China therefore carries risks, the United States should also make a strong commitment to cooperating with China and other states of the region should Kim Jong-Il's regime implode. Beijing should understand that the nuclear crisis provides China with a major opportunity to enhance its role as an American partner in East Asia.

6. *Interim measures to test North Korea.* Although a strategy designed to achieve a comprehensive settlement of the nuclear issue and the normalization of relations is the best mid-term course for the United States, several critical short-term goals can be better attained through a more limited preliminary agreement.

The terms of a preliminary agreement should call for limited concessions by both sides. The North should freeze its reactors (both operational and those under construction) and known reprocessing facilities. The North would also be required to readmit inspectors and account for and turn over all spent nuclear fuel rods as well as any plutonium that may have separated from those rods. The United States and its partners, in return, should resume KEDO heavy fuel oil shipments. The United States should provide formal assurances to North Korea that it will not attack the North and should agree not to object to foreign assistance by other countries as long as the interim agreement remains in effect. Such a preliminary agreement would not address all U.S. security concerns (or meet all North Korean demands). It should be followed by talks aimed at a more comprehensive settlement.

The objectives of a preliminary arrangement would be fourfold. First, by putting a limited but concrete proposal on the table, the United States would test the North and help determine if Pyongyang is serious about negotiations or simply using talks as a smokescreen behind which it will pursue its nuclear program. Second, a preliminary agreement could, depending on its design, slow further deterioration of the situation. Third, positive results would restore some confidence on each side about its ability to deal constructively with the other. And fourth, by demonstrating seriousness of purpose to U.S. allies and other partners, the negotiations would strengthen America's ability to secure commitments from them in support of a larger settlement.

CONTINGENCY OPTIONS

What If Negotiations Fail?
As indicated earlier, North Korea may have decided to acquire a more substantial nuclear weapons capability, and it may try to use negotiations to buy time to produce nuclear weapons. It is also possible that North Korea wants a negotiated settlement of security issues but only on terms that the United States cannot or should not agree to (e.g., without tough inspection provisions).

In the event that the United States makes a concerted and serious effort at negotiations and those efforts fail, the United States should pursue two options:

First, it should demand that China, South Korea, Japan, Russia, and others suspend aid to and trade with North Korea—except for food and medical aid, which should be specifically exempted on humanitarian grounds. If the United States has secured assurances for follow-up action by its regional partners under an integrated strategy, as the Task Force suggests above, Washington should hold those states to account. If some balk, the United States should consider introducing a sanctions proposal in the United Nations and force them to take a clear position.

Second, the United States should, depending on circumstances, consult with its regional partners and consider establishing a blockade of the coast of North Korea designed to prevent fissile material or nuclear weapons from being exported out of the country. The United States could declare that, as part of this effort, it will seize other contraband exports, including drugs, counterfeit money, and missiles. If the United States decides to undertake a blockade, it should try to ensure that Russia and China carry out the strictest border regulations, including measures to closely screen all North Korean aircraft and ships landing and docking within their respective national territories. Even with such support from regional states—and certainly without it—the fact that plutonium is small, easy to transport, and difficult to detect makes it impossible to guarantee that any blockade could successfully interdict plutonium exports.

Clearly, either of these measures, especially the second, could spark war. The United States will have to decide whether it is prepared to go down this path and if so, how much support it will need. The Task Force emphasizes that the "failure" of negotiations cannot be announced hastily or perfunctorily, and it is not providing an endorsement for an early transition to this approach without first exhausting the strategy discussed in this report. If negotiations have truly failed, however, the United States should consider moving forward with these tough measures to the extent possible, even without the full support of its regional partners. Any decision of such importance must be made based on the circumstances of the time.

What If North Korea Reprocesses Spent Fuel?

U.S. intelligence now believes that North Korea in recent days may already have separated small amounts of plutonium from its spent nuclear fuel rods and that it may be preparing to open its full-scale reprocessing facility at Yongbyon.

If it is confirmed that North Korea is reprocessing, then the time available for a peaceful settlement will be short. The United States should notify North Korea that it must be prepared to halt all further reprocessing and make all of its spent fuel rods and separated plutonium available for careful inspection or face serious consequences. If North Korea fails to take the necessary actions, the United States should end any ongoing negotiations and consider some of the measures above.

Should North Korea be immediately willing to submit its spent fuel to inspection and ship its plutonium out of the country—as well as meet the other requirements discussed above as part of an interim agreement—the United States should reciprocate with the conditional security guarantees already discussed. In other words, if North Korea is willing to quickly undo the damage done, the United States should use the opportunity to seal an interim agreement.

A strict time limit should be imposed on this effort from the start, with the period determined by the method the North is pursuing in its reprocessing. It should be understood that if the North reprocesses, any prospect for resolving the crisis diplomatically will have narrowed enormously.

Military Strikes on Nuclear Facilities?

The United States should not rule out strikes on North Korean nuclear facilities, except as part of an agreement and only for as long as the North remains in compliance with the agreement's terms. But this option carries immense risks and uncertainties, and we believe it should only be considered under a very narrow range of circumstances.

The problems associated with a military strike are legion. No matter how well designed the attack is, there can be no guarantee that radiation will not be released into the atmosphere. The United States can only hit those targets it can find. These include the reprocessing facility at Yongbyon as well as all nuclear reactors. More than likely, however, U.S. troops would not find, much less bury or destroy, North Korea's stockpile of spent fuel, from which plutonium could be extracted at a later date. Nor could the United States be certain that there are no secondary or alternative reprocessing facilities located elsewhere; in fact it is likely that at least one additional small-scale facility capable of extracting plutonium does exist. An attack is unlikely to eliminate any existing nuclear weapons. And it would probably prove impossible to target facilities for enriching uranium. Hence, military strikes could delay the acquisition of additional nuclear weapons, but they could not stop that eventuality from occurring.

At the same time, the costs and risks would be high. Although other actions, such as full-scale sanctions and especially a naval blockade, might conceivably incite an attack by North Korea, actual military strikes would be far more likely to bring about such an outcome. Given the dangers to North Korea of a full-scale war, it may well respond with limited counterstrikes rather than an invasion of South Korea. But considering the uncertainties involved in estimating North Korean intentions and the proximity of opposing forces, much-larger-scale combat is a real possibility.

Conclusion

Many people expected the United States would one day again face a quandary similar to that faced in 1994, but most expected the crisis to arrive when North Korea had to come clean on its plutonium program under the Agreed Framework. The arrival of the crisis was speeded up by North Korea's pursuit of an HEU program. Much about the current crisis is similar to 1994. Pyongyang is once again resorting to escalation, even as it expresses interest in negotiating with the United States (and on many occasions has signaled the specific terms it seeks). How serious it is about actually halting its nuclear program again remains to be seen. The alliance is still divided on how to respond. South Korea is once more opposed to any "tough" option, even more so than in 1994. Nor, as in 1994, have the allies arrived at a concerted approach.

There are also important differences from the 1994 crisis. North Korea has asserted it has nuclear weapons, making a rollback immensely more difficult. North Korea is also weaker and has little prospect of reversing its decline without major foreign aid and an internal overhaul. In addition, it has lost enormous credibility because of its secret HEU program, and it is isolated from the international community. The United States has shown little inclination to seriously engage North Korea and for the duration of the Iraq crisis put the problem on something of a back burner. The United States has issued no threats to use force as it did in 1994; quite the contrary. China is playing a more cooperative role than it did previously and now is more concerned about the potential ramifications of North Korea's nuclear program.

A negotiated settlement that meets U.S. needs is of course desirable, but it is unclear whether such an agreement can be achieved. It is arguable whether delay in testing North Korean intentions works toward achieving the goal of an agreement, or whether instead it leads to escalation. Most countries believe the latter to be the case; so does the Task Force.

North Korea's secret pursuit of an HEU program in violation of the Agreed Framework is hardly an inducement to another set of negotiations with Pyongyang. The Bush administration is right to be skeptical. But if left alone, North Korea may produce additional nuclear capabilities, a development that could have fearsome consequences. The United States and its regional partners must do everything they can to put an end to the North's nuclear program. Conceivably, North Korea's increasingly provocative behavior and rhetoric will unite all U.S. partners and move them to say, "Enough is enough." But we are skeptical that unity can be achieved without the United States having seriously pursued negotiations with the North. "Serious" in this case means a willingness to trade real benefits, not simply to demand the moon. Both bilateral and multilateral requirements and benefits are needed. The Task Force believes it is time to swiftly achieve allied consensus on policy and initiate a serious dialogue with North Korea in both bilateral and multilateral fora. Such talks cannot realistically be avoided if the United States wants to mobilize its allies to deal effectively with the nuclear issue. If negotiations fail, the stage will have been set for tougher action by the United States and its regional partners, albeit with correspondingly higher risks.

ADDITIONAL AND DISSENTING VIEWS

On Japan's Position

Japan remains unprepared for a potential crisis on the Korean Peninsula. No serious planning has been done by any agency of the government for worst-case scenarios, and the problem posed by
North Korea's links to Japan—both through organized crime
and the political world—has never been adequately addressed. The
prime minister should convene a group composed of key Diet members, top officials from all the relevant agencies of the Japanese government, and outside experts to tackle both issues forthrightly.

Daniel E. Bob

On the Question of Bilateral or Multilateral Negotiations

Although the United States must be willing to actively and sin-
cerely participate in multilateral negotiations with North Korea,
I believe that the time for bilateral U.S.-DPRK talks has passed.
North Korea's withdrawal from the nuclear Nonproliferation
Treaty (NPT) and its recent declaration to U.S. negotiators that
it has nuclear weapons are possibly part of an attempt to pursue
a nuclear breakout scenario similar to that of Pakistan's. The risk
is that North Korea's short-term tactical objective is to force or entice
the United States into bilateral talks, which would in the current
environment implicitly recognize North Korea as a nuclear state,
thus undermining ongoing efforts to halt the deterioration of
the global nonproliferation regime. Should the United States
enter into bilateral talks while North Korea continues to declare
its nuclear status, the North might then stall the talks for a matter of months, thus potentially riding out what could be the worst
period of international reaction to its nuclear declarations and ambi-
tions. By the time such bilateral talks end or collapse, the focus

would likely be on the mutual recriminations as to who was responsible for the breakdown of the talks rather than on the acceptability of North Korea's withdrawal from the NPT and its declarations of its nuclear status. The momentum and the international solidarity required to deny North Korea's bid to become a nuclear power will have been broken. If the current crisis is to be solved peacefully, it will require the international community to speak with a unified voice. Although North Korea may still not respond to a unified multilateral approach, a sincere U.S. attempt at forging such an approach is essential if the United States is to gain the support of China, South Korea, and Japan in responding to the less favorable scenarios that may lie ahead.

L. Gordon Flake

On the Importance of Negotiations
Significant progress with North Korea will only be achieved through sustained talks and negotiations. Sporadic meetings with inflexible demands and agendas will not do the job.

Donald P. Gregg

On Military Strikes
I agree with the Task Force report—with one exception. I do not agree with one of the contingency options. The United States should not contemplate striking North Korean nuclear facilities under any circumstances. The consequences of such a strike would be unfathomable, as the report itself points out.

Joseph M. Ha

On a Naval Blockade
I am concerned about the international legal ramifications of a naval quarantine of North Korea without UN support or the support

of the states on the North Korean perimeter: China, South Korea, and Russia. Those states might agree to an embargo if it is limited to fissile material and had UN support. Obtaining Chinese backing for such action is extremely important, given China's role in providing critical support to the North Korean defense industrial base.

Richard Kessler

On Missiles, Multilateralism, and Sequence

I have signed this report because it contains much good analysis and some useful recommendations. Its thoughtful treatment of exceedingly difficult issues should contribute to the national debate on one of America's most daunting international challenges. Nevertheless, I wish to emphasize my serious disagreements with some of the policy prescriptions.

Missiles. The report should have made clear that this threat, in addition to the nuclear one, needs to be addressed on an urgent basis. This is crucial for Japan, not to mention Hawaii and Alaska.

Multilateralism. I fully support the Bush administration's emphasis on a multilateral approach and solution. That is the only way to provide the necessary pressures, incentives, and guarantees for North Korea. All the regional powers have major stakes in these issues and should be involved.

The report's recommendation of parallel multilateral and bilateral tracks would lead to North Korea focusing on the bilateral route, while at best it went through the motions in any multilateral forum. The other regional partners would be tempted to go along with this fig leaf of multilateralism.

I believe there should be only one negotiating framework and that it must be multilateral. At a minimum, this means four powers (including South Korea as well as China), though it would be preferable to include Japan and Russia as well. Within such a framework, bilateral talks of various kinds could take place. But then the

U.S.-North Korean dialogue would occur with the discipline of multilateral pressures, incentives, and guarantees.

Sequence. The report is vague on the sequence of moves by North Korea and the United States, but simultaneity is clearly implied. I believe North Korea must take the first steps on its nuclear program—it cannot be "paid" once again for honoring agreements it violated. The United States could make clear what it would be prepared to do (e.g., some form of security assurance) once North Korea has completely fulfilled its obligations. This should be the sequential process on both interim measures and at least some of any fuller agreements. Given its track record, North Korea must move first. But it would do so knowing that the United States would respond, a commitment guaranteed by the other powers.

Winston Lord

On a Naval Blockade
I agree in general terms with the report but do not endorse its recommendations about a naval blockade. Although measures such as a blockade may have to be considered if negotiations do not succeed, I do not believe it is either necessary or wise to voice approval of them at this stage without much more serious consideration of their potentially grave consequences and of possible alternative courses of action than the Task Force has undertaken.

Donald Oberdorfer
joined by
Edward J. Baker

On a Naval Blockade
I respectfully dissent from some of the recommendations in the section on "Contingency Options."

The idea that the United States could establish a naval blockade of the North Korean coast to ensure that Pyongyang does not export any fissile material or nuclear weapons is a dangerous delusion. For how long, exactly, should the United States maintain this blockade? A few months? Years? Forever? And all the while North Korea continues to add to its nuclear arsenal? Further, simple geography indicates that land borders would also need to be secured; the hundreds of refugees and migrant workers that cross daily from North Korea into China give some sense of the challenge here. And there is no guarantee that other key countries in the region would play along. In short, a blockade would not prevent the North from increasing its nuclear stockpile, and it would not give us any confidence that fissile materials or nuclear weapons were not being exported.

In addition, Pyongyang has declared that any such action would be tantamount to war. Whether it would make good on this threat is unclear, but it must be taken seriously. This means that U.S. forces in the South would have to be reinforced beforehand, a step that would likely cause great tension in the South Korean-American alliance. The report does not consider this aspect of the problem.

When dealing with North Korea, it is often tempting to shy away from hard truths because the reality is so disagreeable. The fact is that North Korea may soon acquire a significant nuclear arsenal with the potential to export bombs around the globe, including to terrorist organizations. This may well justify the United States having to change the Kim Jong-Il regime through military means. Before we reach that point, though, it would be useful to learn if we could change the way the regime behaves through diplomatic means.

Mitchell B. Reiss

On Negotiations and the Terms of an Interim Agreement
I agree with those who caution about the dangers of escalation arising out of interdiction. Realistically, however, it is highly likely that some level of quarantine will be imposed if the North continues to up the ante. The lesson there, however, is that the United States needs to avoid getting to that point by engaging seriously

with the DPRK and abandoning the notion that negotiation is either a reward or concession. Although the terms of any agreement need not—should not—"pay" the North for restoring the status quo ante by ending the HEU program and refreezing the plutonium program, it would be irresponsible for the United States to continue insisting that it will discuss the terms of a broader agreement—one including total dismantlement of the nuclear program in exchange for security guarantees and related steps—only after the North acts first, unilaterally.

In this regard, the Task Force report is somewhat unclear regarding the handling of spent fuel canned and stored under the 1994 Agreed Framework (or created by renewed operation of the five-megawatt reactor). Under the terms of any full, final agreement described by the Task Force, that spent fuel must be shipped out of the country soon, as opposed to waiting until just before the key nuclear components of the first light-water reactor are to be delivered (as the Agreed Framework specified). However, under the terms of the *interim agreement* the report calls for during negotiations, while that spent fuel would be placed once again under international monitoring and supervision, it would remain in North Korea. This is far from ideal, as it leaves the situation open to yet another round of gamesmanship on reprocessing. But it is unrealistic to expect the North to agree to an irreversible requirement for accelerated removal of the spent fuel as a price for merely negotiating.

Alan D. Romberg

On China's Responsibilities and Partisan Overtones
The Korea Task Force report deserves credit for its comprehensive approach to the vexing challenges posed by North Korea's nuclear weapons program and readiness to violate and renounce past agreements. I would have liked to join the consensus but cannot do so.

Although I agree that the United States should take the lead in achieving a common coalition strategy to preclude definitively a North Korea that is, or seeks to be, nuclear armed, I believe that the burdens inherent in such a strategy should not fall disproportionately on the United States. China, in particular, has at least as great a stake in a fully, verifiably denuclearized North Korea as does the United States. I do not believe that it is in the interest of the United States to again be singled out by North Korea as the only party with which it will deal. I also deplore the partisan overtones in the references to the Bush administration.

Helmut Sonnenfeldt

On China's Position
"China prefers low-profile diplomacy, and the role the United States has bestowed on Beijing during the current crisis is not necessarily a welcome one," the report states.

Although I agree with this as one side of Beijing's view, it also appears to be the case that having been thrust into this position, the Chinese are now quite pleased with the credit they have been given for convening the meeting and playing a constructive part in advancing a dialogue.

Nancy Bernkopf Tucker

TASK FORCE MEMBERS

MORTON I. ABRAMOWITZ is a Senior Fellow at the Century Foundation. He was U.S. Ambassador to Thailand and has served as the President of the Carnegie Endowment for International Peace.

DESAIX ANDERSON is former Executive Director of the Korean Peninsula Energy Development Organization.

EDWARD J. BAKER* is Associate Director of the Harvard-Yenching Institute, a foundation associated with Harvard University that brings East Asian scholars to the United States for research and studies.

DANIEL E. BOB* is Council on Foreign Relations Hitachi International Affairs Fellow in Japan and Research Adviser to Japan's National Institute for Research Advancement.

STEPHEN W. BOSWORTH is Dean of the Fletcher School at Tufts University. He has served as U.S. Ambassador to the Republic of Korea and the Philippines.

VICTOR D. CHA is an Associate Professor of Government at the Edmund A. Walsh School of Foreign Service, Georgetown University.

JEROME A. COHEN is Adjunct Senior Fellow for Asia Studies at the Council on Foreign Relations. He is also counsel to the international law firm of Paul, Weiss, Rifkind, Wharton & Garrison and is Professor of Law at New York University Law School.

Note: Task Force members participate in their individual and not institutional capacities.

*The individual has endorsed the report and submitted an additional or a dissenting view.

JAMES E. DELANEY is a consultant at the Institute for Defense Analyses. He served as a U.S. intelligence officer in Asia for more than twenty years.

L. GORDON FLAKE* is Executive Director of the Maureen and Mike Mansfield Foundation. Formerly, he was Associate Director of the Program on Conflict Resolution at the Atlantic Council of the United States.

DONALD P. GREGG* is Chairman of The Korea Society in New York. He served as the Central Intelligence Agency Station Chief in Seoul (1973–75) and as Ambassador to the Republic of Korea (1989–93).

JOSEPH M. HA* is Vice President of International Business and Government Relations at Nike, Inc. He is also Professor Emeritus at Lewis and Clark College.

ERIC HEGINBOTHAM is Senior Fellow in Asia Studies at the Council on Foreign Relations.

FRANK S. JANNUZI is a Democratic Staff Member on the Senate Foreign Relations Committee. He served as an East Asia regional political-military analyst in the Bureau of Intelligence and Research, Department of State.

RICHARD KESSLER* is the Democratic Staff Director of the Subcommittee on Financial Management, the Budget, and International Security for the Senate Committee on Governmental Affairs.

SUKHAN KIM is Senior Partner at Akin, Gump, Strauss, Hauer & Feld. He is also the Founder and President of the Sukhan Kim Foundation: Korean-American Youth Service Organization, Inc.

JAMES T. LANEY is President Emeritus of Emory University. He served as U.S. Ambassador to the Republic of Korea (1993–97).

KENNETH G. LIEBERTHAL is Professor of Political Science and the William Davidson Professor of Business Administration at the University of Michigan. He served as Senior Director of Asia at the National Security Council (1998–2000).

WINSTON LORD* is Co-Chairman of the International Rescue Committee. He served as Assistant Secretary of State for East Asian and Pacific Affairs and Ambassador to China.

K. A. NAMKUNG is an independent consultant specializing in U.S.-Asian relations. He advises government agencies and businesses in the United States and East Asia.

MARCUS NOLAND is a Senior Fellow at the Institute for International Economics. He has served as the Senior Economist for International Economics at the Council of Economic Advisers.

DONALD OBERDORFER* is Distinguished Journalist-in-Residence and an Adjunct Professor at the Nitze School of Advanced International Studies, The Johns Hopkins University. He is also the author of *The Two Koreas: A Contemporary History*.

KONGDAN OH is a Research Staff Member at the Institute for Defense Analyses and a Nonresident Senior Fellow at the Brookings Institution.

MITCHELL B. REISS* is Dean of International Affairs at the College of William and Mary. He has served as Assistant Executive Director and Senior Policy Adviser at the Korean Peninsula Energy Development Organization.

ROBERT W. RISCASSI is a retired U.S. Army General. He has served as Commander in Chief of UN Command and Commander in Chief of the Republic of Korea-U.S. Combined Forces Command.

---

*The individual has endorsed the report and submitted an additional or a dissenting view.

ALAN D. ROMBERG* is Senior Associate at the Henry L. Stimson Center. He served as Principal Deputy Director of the State Department's Policy Planning Staff under President Clinton.

JASON T. SHAPLEN was a Policy Adviser at the Korean Peninsula Energy Development Organization (KEDO) (1995–99), where his primary responsibility was to prepare and negotiate agreements between KEDO and North Korea.

WENDY R. SHERMAN is a principal at The Albright Group. She served as a Counselor of the Department of State, with the rank of Ambassador during the Clinton administration.

SCOTT SNYDER is the Korea Representative at The Asia Foundation. He is the author of *Negotiating on the Edge: North Korean Negotiating Behavior*.

STEPHEN J. SOLARZ heads an international business consultancy. He was also Vice Chair at the International Crisis Group. For twelve of his eighteen years in the House of Representatives, he served as Chairman of the Subcommittee on Asian and Pacific Affairs.

NANCY BERNKOPF TUCKER* is Professor of History at Georgetown University in the Edmund A. Walsh School of Foreign Service. She served in the State Department Office of Chinese Affairs and the U.S. Embassy, Beijing (1986–87).

WILLIAM WATTS is President of Potomac Associates. He has served as U.S. Foreign Service Officer in the Republic of Korea, Germany, and the Soviet Union, and as Staff Secretary at the National Security Council.

JOEL WIT is a Senior Fellow at the Center for Strategic and International Studies.

DONALD S. ZAGORIA is a Trustee at the National Committee on American Foreign Policy and also a Professor of Government at Hunter College.

MEMBERS NOT CONCURRING WITH THE REPORT

RICHARD V. ALLEN is a Senior Fellow at the Hoover Institution on War, Revolution, and Peace, Stanford University. He served as National Security Adviser to President Ronald W. Reagan.

ROBERT DUJARRIC is a Fellow at the Hudson Institute and chairs the Korea-Japan seminar series.

ARNOLD KANTER is a Principal at the Scowcroft Group. He served as Under Secretary of State for Political Affairs (1991–93) and as Special Assistant to the President for defense policy and arms control (1989–91).

HELMUT SONNENFELDT** is a Guest Scholar for Foreign Policy Studies at the Brookings Institution. He has served as a Senior Staff Member of the National Security Council.

**The individual wrote a dissenting view.

TASK FORCE OBSERVERS

Michael J. Green
National Security Council

Paul C. Grove
Subcommittee on Foreign Operations of the
U.S. Senate Committee on Appropriations

John Merrill
U.S. Department of State

Charles L. Pritchard
U.S. Department of State

SELECTED REPORTS OF INDEPENDENT TASK FORCES
SPONSORED BY THE COUNCIL ON FOREIGN RELATIONS

* †*Emergency Responders: Drastically Underfunded, Dangerously Unprepared* (2003)
  Warren B. Rudman, Chair; Richard A. Clarke, Senior Adviser; Jamie F. Metzl,
  Project Director
* †*Burma: Time for Change* (2003)
  Mathea Falco, Chair
* †*Chinese Military Power* (2003)
  Harold Brown, Chair; Joseph W. Prueher, Vice Chair; Adam Segal,
  Project Director
* †*Iraq: The Day After* (2003)
  Thomas R. Pickering and James R. Schlesinger, Co-Chairs; Eric P.
  Schwartz, Project Director
* †*Threats to Democracy* (2002)
  Madeleine K. Albright and Bronislaw Geremek, Co-Chairs; Morton H.
  Halperin, Project Director; Elizabeth Frawley Bagley, Associate Director
* †*America—Still Unprepared, Still in Danger* (2002)
  Gary Hart and Warren B. Rudman, Co-Chairs; Stephen Flynn, Project Director
* †*Terrorist Financing* (2002)
  Maurice R. Greenberg, Chair; William F. Wechsler and Lee S. Wolosky, Project
  Co-Directors
* †*Enhancing U.S. Leadership at the United Nations* (2002)
  David Dreier and Lee H. Hamilton, Co-Chairs; Lee Feinstein and Adrian Karat-
  nycky, Project Co-Directors
* †*Testing North Korea: The Next Stage in U.S. and ROK Policy (2001)*
  Morton I. Abramowitz and James T. Laney, Co-Chairs; Robert A. Manning,
  Project Director
* †*The United States and Southeast Asia: A Policy Agenda for the New Administration*
  (2001)
  J. Robert Kerrey, Chair; Robert A. Manning, Project Director
* †*Strategic Energy Policy: Challenges for the 21st Century* (2001)
  Edward L. Morse, Chair; Amy Myers Jaffe, Project Director
* †*State Department Reform* (2001)
  Frank C. Carlucci, Chair; Ian J. Brzezinski, Project Coordinator;
  Cosponsored with the Center for Strategic and International Studies
* †*U.S.-Cuban Relations in the 21st Century: A Follow-on Report* (2001)
  Bernard W. Aronson and William D. Rogers, Co-Chairs; Julia Sweig and Walter
  Mead, Project Directors
* †*A Letter to the President and a Memorandum on U.S. Policy Toward Brazil* (2001)
  Stephen Robert, Chair; Kenneth Maxwell, Project Director
* †*Toward Greater Peace and Security in Colombia* (2000)
  Bob Graham and Brent Scowcroft, Co-Chairs; Michael Shifter, Project Director;
  Cosponsored with the Inter-American Dialogue
  †*Future Directions for U.S. Economic Policy Toward Japan* (2000)
  Laura D'Andrea Tyson, Chair; M. Diana Helweg Newton, Project Director
* †*Promoting Sustainable Economies in the Balkans* (2000)
  Steven Rattner, Chair; Michael B. G. Froman, Project Director
* †*Nonlethal Technologies: Progress and Prospects* (1999)
  Richard L. Garwin, Chair; W. Montague Winfield, Project Director
* †*U.S. Policy Toward North Korea: Next Steps* (1999)
  Morton I. Abramowitz and James T. Laney, Co-Chairs; Michael J. Green, Project
  Director
  †*Safeguarding Prosperity in a Global Financial System: The Future International Finan-
  cial Architecture* (1999)
  Carla A. Hills and Peter G. Peterson, Co-Chairs; Morris Goldstein, Project
  Director

---

†Available on the Council on Foreign Relations website at www.cfr.org.
*Available from Brookings Institution Press. To order, call 800-275-1447.